PLAY GUITAR W  2
(1988-1991)

Wise Publications
part of The Music Sales Group
London/New York/Paris/Sydney/Copenhagen/Berlin/Madrid/Tokyo

Published by
Wise Publications
8/9 Frith Street, London W1D 3JB, England

Exclusive Distributors:
Music Sales Limited
Distribution Centre, Newmarket Road, Bury St Edmunds, Suffolk IP33 3YB
Music Sales Pty Limited
120 Rothschild Avenue, Rosebery, NSW 2018, Australia

Order No. AM980815
ISBN 1-84449-663-5
This book © Copyright 2004 by Wise Publications

Compiled by Nick Crispin
Music arranged by Arthur Dick
Music processed by Paul Ewers Music Design
Project Editor: Tom Fleming
Printed in the United Kingdom

CD recorded, mixed and mastered by
John Rose & Jonas Persson
All guitars by Arthur Dick
Bass by Paul Townsend
Drums by Brett Morgan

Your Guarantee of Quality

*As publishers, we strive to produce
every book to the highest commercial standards.
The music has been freshly engraved and the book has
been carefully designed to minimise awkward page turns
and to make playing from it a real pleasure.
Particular care has been given to specifying acid-free,
neutral-sized paper made from pulps which have not been
elemental chlorine bleached. This pulp is from farmed
sustainable forests and was produced with
special regard for the environment.
Throughout, the printing and binding have been planned
to ensure a sturdy, attractive publication which
should give years of enjoyment.
If your copy fails to meet our high standards,
please inform us and we will gladly replace it.*

www.musicsales.com

Guitar Tablature Explained

Guitar music can be notated in three different ways: on a musical stave, in tablature, and in rhythm slashes.

RHYTHM SLASHES are written above the stave. Strum chords in the rhythm indicated. Round noteheads indicate single notes.

THE MUSICAL STAVE shows pitches and rhythms and is divided by lines into bars. Pitches are named after the first seven letters of the alphabet.

TABLATURE graphically represents the guitar fingerboard. Each horizontal line represents a string, and each number represents a fret.

4th string, 2nd fret

1st & 2nd strings open, played together

open D chord

Definitions For Special Guitar Notation

SEMI-TONE BEND: Strike the note and bend up a semi-tone (1/2 step).

WHOLE-TONE BEND: Strike the note and bend up a whole-tone (whole step).

GRACE NOTE BEND: Strike the note and bend as indicated. Play the first note as quickly as possible.

QUARTER-TONE BEND: Strike the note and bend up a 1/4 step.

BEND & RELEASE: Strike the note and bend up as indicated, then release back to the original note.

COMPOUND BEND & RELEASE: Strike the note and bend up and down in the rhythm indicated.

PRE-BEND: Bend the note as indicated, then strike it.

PRE-BEND & RELEASE: Bend the note as indicated. Strike it and release the note back to the original pitch.

UNISON BEND: Strike the two notes simultaneously and bend the lower note up to the pitch of the higher.

BEND & RESTRIKE: Strike the note and bend as indicated then restrike the string where the symbol occurs.

BEND, HOLD AND RELEASE: Same as bend and release but hold the bend for the duration of the tie.

BEND AND TAP: Bend the note as indicated and tap the higher fret while still holding the bend.

VIBRATO: The string is vibrated by rapidly bending and releasing the note with the fretting hand.

HAMMER-ON: Strike the first note with one finger, then sound the second note (on the same string) with another finger by fretting it without picking.

PULL-OFF: Place both fingers on the notes to be sounded, strike the first note and without picking, pull the finger off to sound the second note.

LEGATO SLIDE (GLISS): Strike the first note and then slide the same fret-hand finger up or down to the second note. The second note is not struck.

NOTE: The speed of any bend is indicated by the music notation and tempo.

SHIFT SLIDE (GLISS & RESTRIKE): Same as legato slide, except the second note is struck.

TRILL: Very rapidly alternate between the notes indicated by continuously hammering on and pulling off.

TAPPING: Hammer ("tap") the fret indicated with the pick-hand index or middle finger and pull off to the note fretted by the fret hand.

PICK SCRAPE: The edge of the pick is rubbed down (or up) the string, producing a scratchy sound.

MUFFLED STRINGS: A percussive sound is produced by laying the fret hand across the string(s) without depressing, and striking them with the pick hand.

NATURAL HARMONIC: Strike the note while the fret-hand lightly touches the string directly over the fret indicated.

PINCH HARMONIC: The note is fretted normally and a harmonic is produced by adding the edge of the thumb or the tip of the index finger of the pick hand to the normal pick attack.

HARP HARMONIC: The note is fretted normally and a harmonic is produced by gently resting the pick hand's index finger directly above the indicated fret (in brackets) while plucking the appropriate string.

PALM MUTING: The note is partially muted by the pick hand lightly touching the string(s) just before the bridge.

RAKE: Drag the pick across the strings indicated with a single motion.

TREMOLO PICKING: The note is picked as rapidly and continuously as possible.

ARPEGGIATE: Play the notes of the chord indicated by quickly rolling them from bottom to top.

SWEEP PICKING: Rhythmic downstroke and/or upstroke motion across the strings.

VIBRATO DIVE BAR AND RETURN: The pitch of the note or chord is dropped a specific number of steps (in rhythm) then returned to the original pitch.

VIBRATO BAR SCOOP: Depress the bar just before striking the note, then quickly release the bar.

VIBRATO BAR DIP: Strike the note and then immediately drop a specific number of steps, then release back to the original pitch.

additional musical definitions

(accent)	•	Accentuate note (play it louder).
(accent)	•	Accentuate note with great intensity.
(staccato)	•	Shorten time value of note.
	•	Downstroke
V	•	Upstroke

D.%. al Coda

• Go back to the sign (%), then play until the bar marked *To Coda* ⊕ then skip to the section marked ⊕ *Coda*.

D.C. al Fine

• Go back to the beginning of the song and play until the bar marked *Fine*.

tacet

• Instrument is silent (drops out).

• Repeat bars between signs.

1. 2.

• When a repeated section has different endings, play the first ending only the first time and the second ending only the second time.

NOTE: Tablature numbers in brackets mean:
1. The note is sustained, but a new articulation (such as hammer on or slide) begins.
2. A note may be fretted but not necessarily played.

All I Want Is You

Words & Music by U2

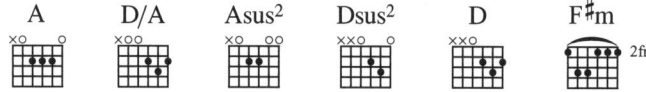

A   D/A   Asus²   Dsus²   D   F#m

Tune all guitars down a semitone

♩ = 92

Intro

A   D/A   A   D/A

1. You

*Gtr. 1 (acous.) + Gtr. 2 (elec.)

cont. sim.

mf   Gtr. 2 (elec.) w/mellow clean tone *p*

*Play Gtr. 2 part

Verse

A   D/A   A   D/A

say   you want___   dia - monds on a ring of   gold.___   You say___

A Asus² A Asus²   D/A   Dsus² D Dsus² D Dsus² A   Asus²   D/A Dsus²   D/A

___   you want___   your sto - ry___ to re - main un - told.___   But all the

6

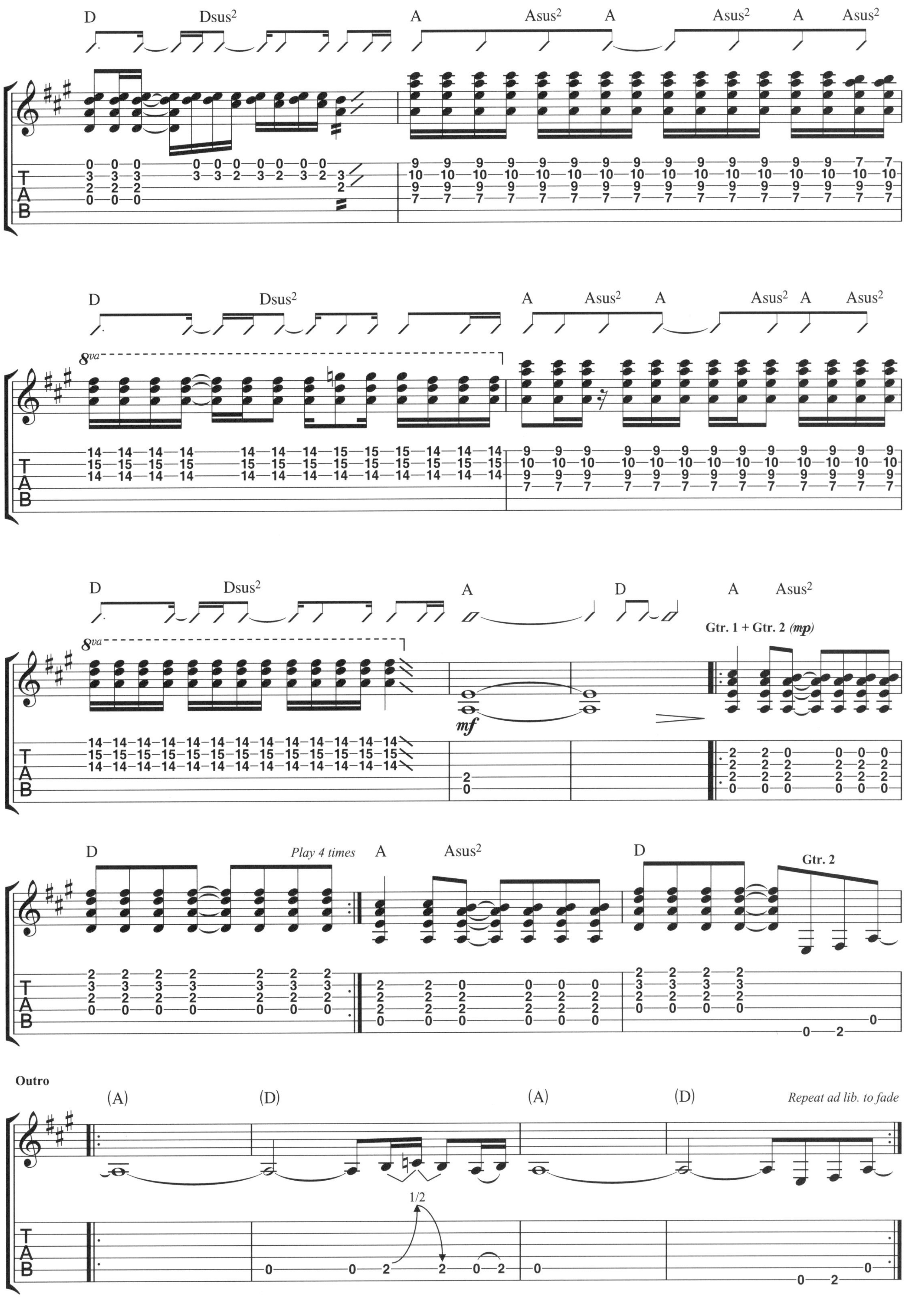

Desire

Words by Bono
Music by U2

sis - ter,_____ I can't let_____ you go._____ Like a

preach - er steal - ing hearts_____ at a tra - vel - ling_____ show. For love or

mo - ney, mo - ney, mo - ney, mo - ney, mo - ney, mo - ney, mo - ney, mo - ney, mo - ney, mo - ney, mo - ney and the

Dsus²   A   Asus² A Asus² A Asus²

fe - ver_____ get - tin' high - er, de -

Gtrs. 1+2+3

Even Better Than The Real Thing

Words & Music by U2

Ah.

1. Give me one

Gtr. 1

Verse *mp*

— more chance and you'll be sa - tis - fied.
(2.) last chance, and I'm gon - na make you sing,

Give me two
give me half

Gtr. 3 w/Fig. 1 *sim.*

— more chan - ces, you won't be de - nied.
a chance to ride on the waves that you bring.

Well my heart
You're ho -

*Gtr. 3 plays ♪'s with chords in ( )

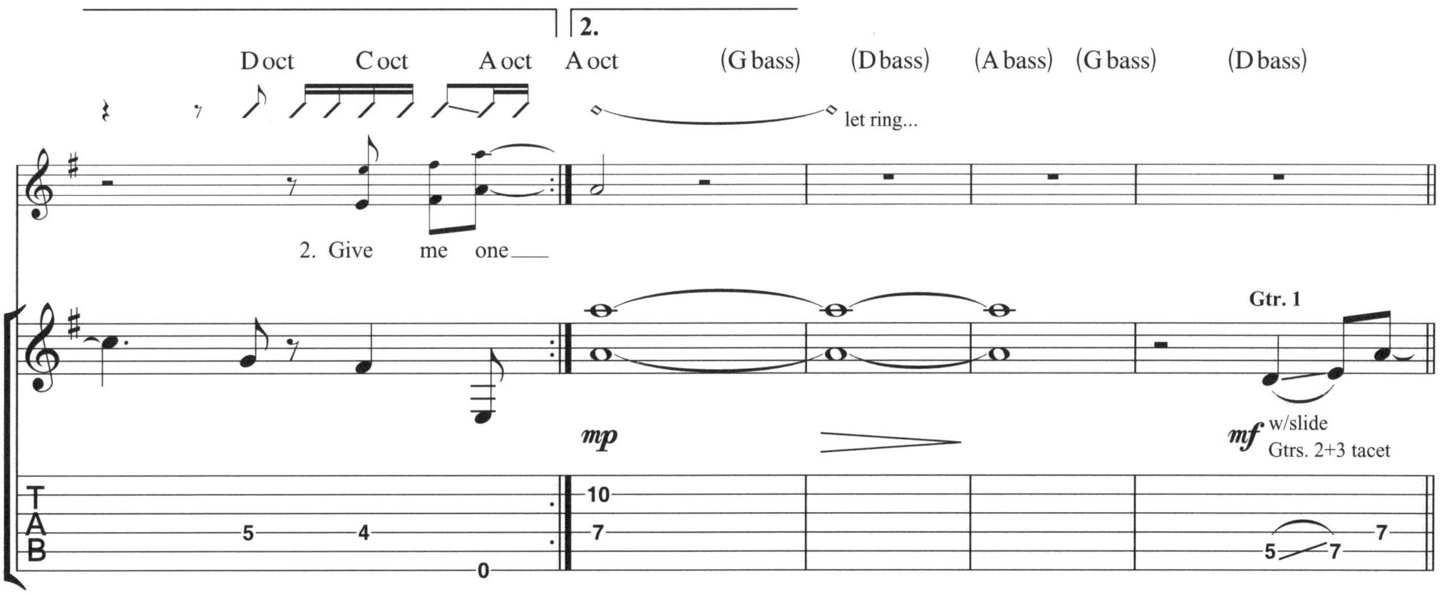

* sound higher 3rd string if using 12 string

Bridge

f w.o/slide
Gtr. 1 w/Fig. 2 (x4)

One

Words & Music by U2

Fmaj7
G
Am
or do you feel the same?
Will it make it ea -
...Fig. 2 ends
Dsus2
Fmaj7
G
- si - er on you, now
you got some - one to blame?
You say
p

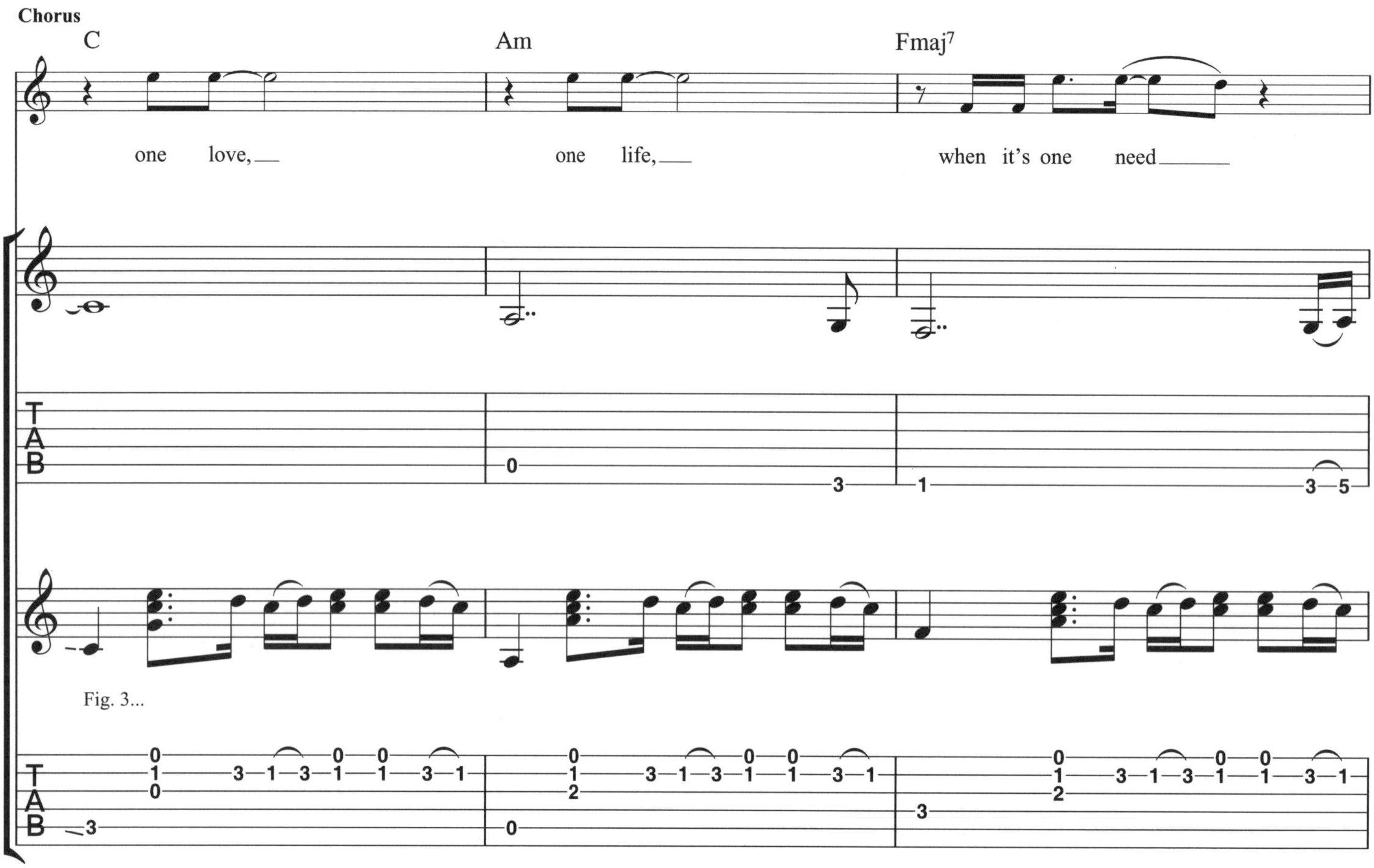

leaves you ba - by if you don't care_____ for it._____

2. Did I dis - ap - point____ you,   or leave a bad__ taste____ in your
3. Have you come here for for - give - ness,   have you__ come to raise the

mouth?   You act____ like you nev - er had love,____
dead?   Have you come here____ to play Je - sus,____

and you__want me__ to go with - out.____   Well__ it's   too late,____
to the le - pers____ in your head?   Did I ask too much,

to - night,___   to drag the past out___ in - to the light.
more than a lot?   You gave me no - thing now it's___ all I got.

We're one,_____ but we're not the same,___ we get___ to
We're one,_____ but we're not the same,___ well___ we

car - ry___ each oth - er,   car - ry___ each oth - er... one._____
hurt___ each oth - er,   then we do it a - gain. You say

1.

Am — Dsus^2 — Fmaj^7 — G

2. Bridge

C — Am — C

Gtr. 3   *cont. sim.*

Gtr. 1

Love is a tem - ple, love a high - er law, love is a tem - ple, love

Am — C

the high - er law. You ask me to en - ter but

G — Fmaj^7

then you make me crawl, and I can't be hold - ing on to what you've got,

(T)

Until The End Of The World

Words & Music by U2

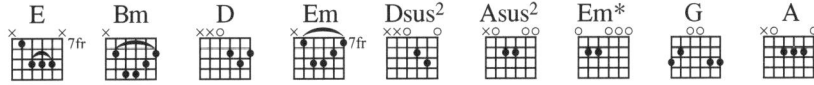

down the hold,_ just   pass-ing   time.__   Last time we met__   it was a

low - lit   room,   we were as__ close to - ge-ther as a   bride and groom.__

We ate__ the food,_   we drank the wine,__   ev-'ry - bo-dy hav-ing a good

Gtr. 3 (elec.)

w/delay

40

G
Dsus2
A
Asus2
A
Asus2
time ex - cept you.
You were talk - ing 'bout the end of the world.

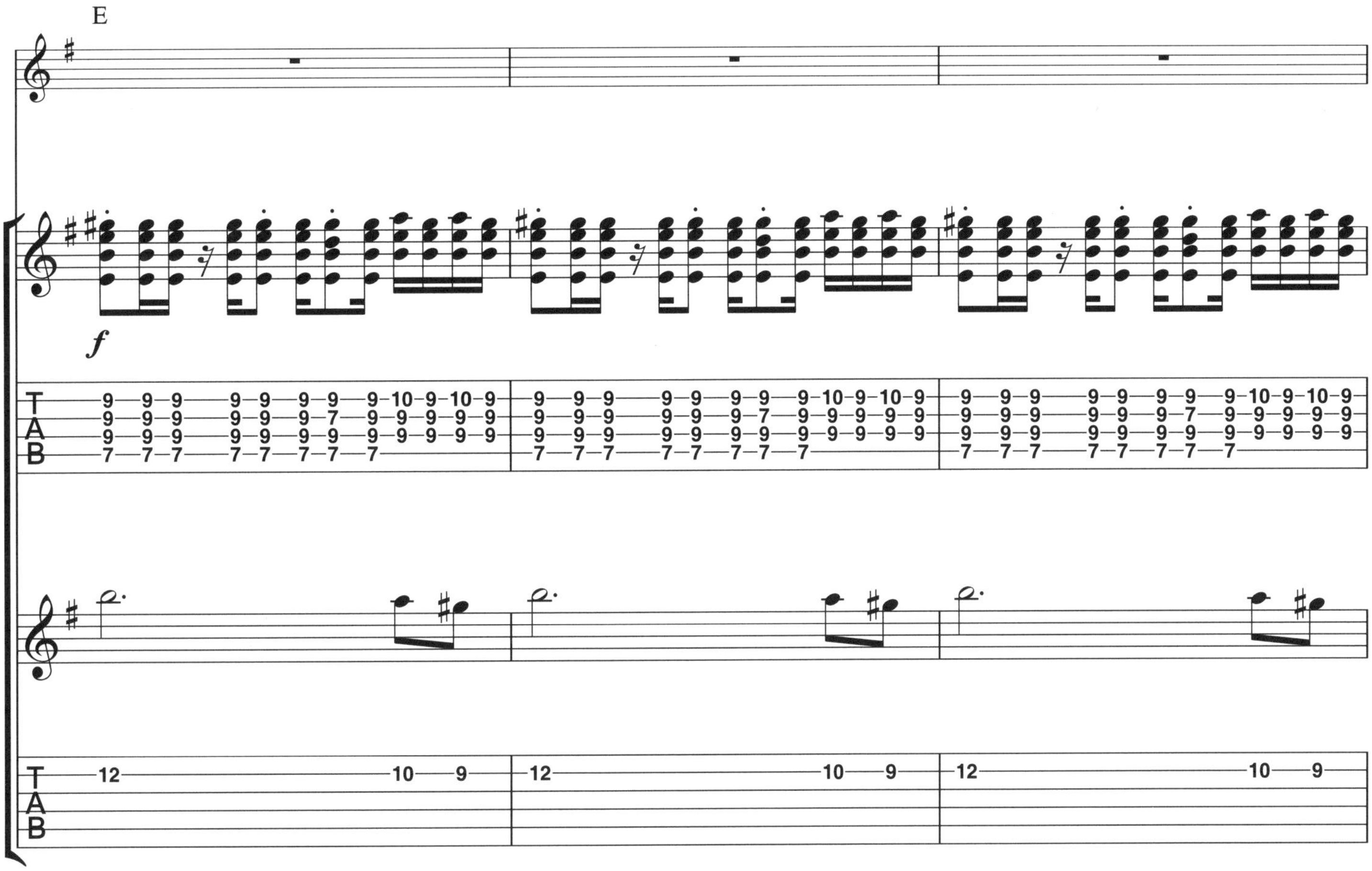
E
f

% Verse

(Bm)

(D)

2. I took the mo - ney, I spiked your drink, you
3. (%) In my dream.___ I was drown - ing my sor - rows, but my

Gtr. 3

8va ----------

Harm. ----------

(Em)

(Bm)

miss too much these___ days if you stop to think.___ You led me on___ with those
sor - rows they___ learned to swim. Sur - round - ing me,___

(8) ----------

Harm. ----------

42

(D)   (Em)

in - no - cent___ eyes,___   you know I love the e - le - ment   of   sur - prise.___
go - ing down___ on me,   spill - ing ov - er the___ brim.

Harm.

Dsus²   Asus⁴   Em*

In   the gar - den   I   was   play - ing the tart,___   I kissed your lips___ and
Waves of re - gret   and   waves of joy,___   I reached out for the___ one   I

let ring…

broke your heart._ You,_ you were act - ing like it was the end_ of the world.
tried to de - stroy._ You,_ you, said you'd_ wait till the end_ of the world.

To Coda ⊕

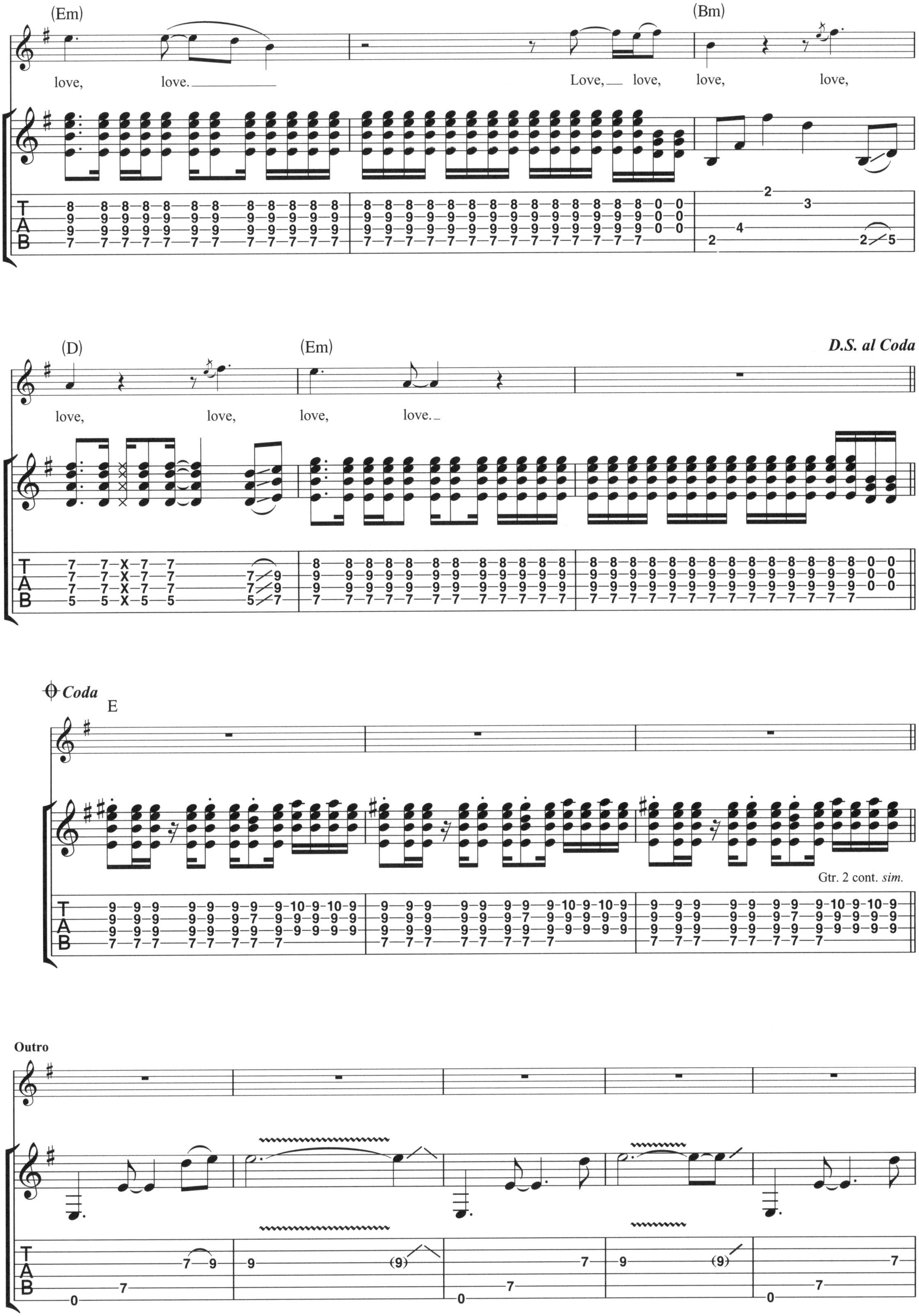

The Fly

Words by Bono
Music by U2

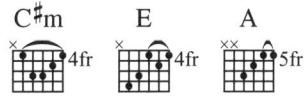

fall - ing from the sky,___ it's no se - cret that our world is in dark - ness to - night. They say the

Harm. -------------------- w/wah --------------------

(A bass)   (D bass)   (E bass)

sun is some - times___ e - clipsed by a moon, you know I don't see you when she

w/bar   w/echo

-1/2

Verse

B   E   G   E   G
⑤   ⑥   ⑤   ⑥   ⑤
2fr   open   10fr   open   10fr

Gtr. 1 (2°)   P.M. ------   P.M. ------
                               Fig. 1 --------------------

walks in the room.   (2.) It's no   se - cret   that a friend___   is some - one who lets___ you help,___   it's no
                      (3.) se - cret   that a con - science   can some - times be___ a pest,___   it's no

Gtr. 1 (1°)

w/open wah
2° play slashes

(A bass)

se - cret that a liar___ won't be - lieve___ in a - ny - one else. They say a se - cret is some - thing you
se - cret am - bi - tion___ bites the nails of suc - cess. Ev - 'ry ar - tist is a canni - bal, ev'ry

Gtr. 2 w/Fig. 1 (x6)

```
7--7--X-7--X-7--7--5          7--7--X-7--X-7----7          7--7--X-7----X-7--7--5
0                           0                    5          0
```

(D bass)   (E bass)

tell one oth - er per - son, so I'm tell - ing___ you___ child.
po - et is a thief, all kill their in - spi - ra - tion and sing a - bout their grief.

cancel wah

```
7--7--X-7--0--5--7--9  (9)    7--X-7--X-7--7--5          7--7--X-7----X-7--7--5--7
0                         0                            0
```

Chorus C#m   E   A

1°+2° (Love_____ we shine like a burn - ing star,___ we're fall -

mp

```
4    4    5
5    5    5
6    4    6
```

- ing from the sky___   C#m   E
A man_ will_ beg,___ a man_ will_ crawl___ on the sheer face_ of
A man_ will_ rise,___ a man_ will_ fall___ to - from the sheer face_ of

```
4    4
5    5
6    4
```

love, like a fly on a wall.___ it's___ no se-cret.___
love, like a fly from a wall,___ it's no se-cret at all.___

Chorus

(C#m) (E) (A)

Love_____ we shine like a burn - ing star___ fall-

(C#m) (E) (A)

- ing from the sky_____ to - night._____

(C#m) (E)

___ Love_____ we shine like a burn-

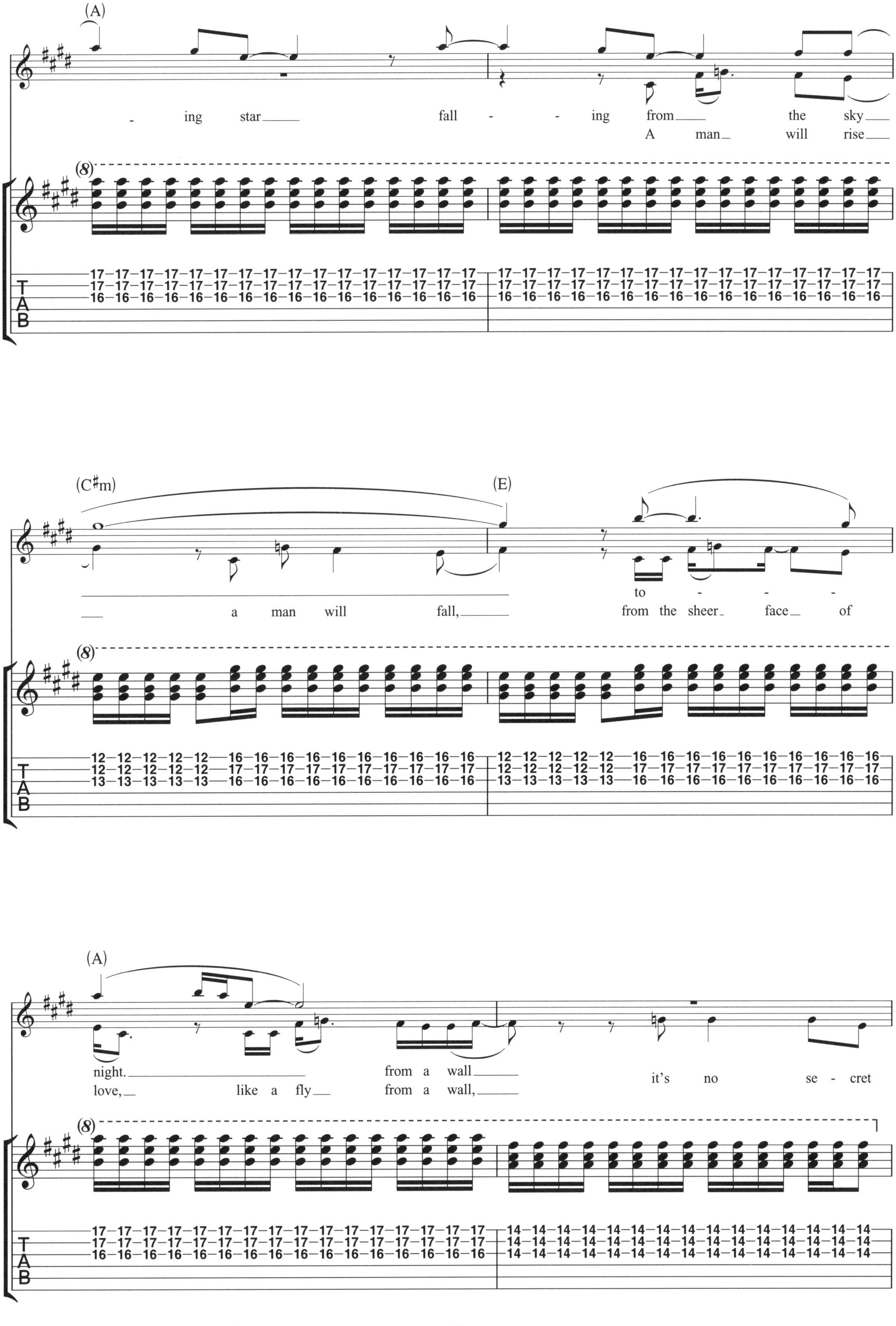

at all.

Oh yeah,___ it's no se - cret that the stars___ are

fall - ing from___ the sky,___ the u - ni - verse___ ex - plod - ing 'cause of

one man's lie.___ Look___ I got - ta go.___ Yeah,___ I'm

run - ning out - ta change.   There's a   lot of things___   if___ I

Outro

could   I'd   re - ar - range.

Mysterious Ways

Words by Bono
Music by U2

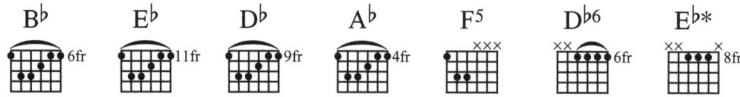

Lyrics:

1. John-ny take a walk with your sis-ter the moon, let her pale light in, to fill up your room. You've been liv-ing un-der-ground, eat-

2. John-ny take a dive with your sis-ter in the rain,_ let her talk a-bout the things you can't ex - plain._ To touch_ is to heal to hurt

(E♭)
(B♭)
(F)
(B♭)
- ing from a can,_ you've been run-ning a - way_ from what you don't un-der stand._
__ is to steal, if you want to kiss the sky, bet - ter learn how to kneel. On your knees boy!
Pre-chorus
B♭
E♭
B♭
*Gtr. 1
She's slip - py, you're slid - ing down, she'll be_ there when you
She's the wave, she turns the tide, she sees a man_ in - side the
Gtrs. 1+2
mf
Gtr. 2
Gtr. 1 cont. in slashes
*play Gtr. 1 part
E♭
Chorus
B♭
Gtr. 2
E♭
D♭
cont. sim.
hit the ground. It's al - right, it's al - right,_ it's al - right. She moves in mys-
child.
Gtr. 1
cont. in slashes

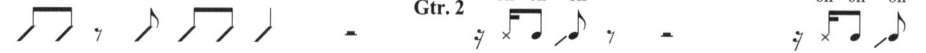

-te-ri-ous ways. It's al-right, it's al-right,— it's al-right. She moves— in mys-

1.

-te-ri-ous ways, ah.——

Gtr. 2

Gtr. 1

w/wah

2.

-te-ri-ous ways,— yeah. It's al-right, it's al-right,— al-right.

Gtr. 2

(E♭bass)

Bridge D♭6   E♭*

One   day   you'll   look_____   back____   and   you'll   see____

D♭6   A♭

_____   where_____   you   were   held_____   now____   by   this   love.____

It's al - right,___ it's al - right,___ al - right.

She moves___ in mys - te - ri - ous ways,___ oh.

Does it move_ you? She moves_ with it.___

Lift my days and light up my nights, oh.___

Gtr. 1

Gtr. 2 cont. *sim.*

w/drums to fade

123456789